March Madness

JUSTICE PREVAILS

authorHOUSE®

AuthorHouse™
1663 Liberty Drive
Bloomington, IN 47403
www.authorhouse.com
Phone: 833-262-8899

Published by AuthorHouse 06/27/2022

ISBN: 978-1-6655-6382-6 (sc)
ISBN: 978-1-6655-6381-9 (e)

Library of Congress Control Number: 2022912093

Print information available on the last page.

Any people depicted in stock imagery provided by Getty Images are models,
and such images are being used for illustrative purposes only.
Certain stock imagery © Getty Images.

This book is printed on acid-free paper.

Thank God Chihuahuas aren't the size of German shepherds

The longer I stay single the more love I have stored up
Brace yourself

Being under the influence of Holy Spirit glorifies God
being under the influence of drugs and alcohol, glorifies
you know who

This virus makes some want to scream like Prince, towards the end of "When Doves Cry"

Hearts can be like snowflakes, unique and different from one another and cold

Sharpie finally made a gel ink pen
now my poems will be deeper and darker

When a parent can't find their child they panic and go look for them
when and addicts brain can't find it substance it panics and is out there looking for it

One two three four I declare a thumb war
the human psyche is saturated with Warfare

Poetry, Poet-Tree
What if there was a tree that grew poets, the kids probably wouldn't steal from it, and the squirrels would be perplexed

3

Michael Jordan once said
"I'm not a poet".....and there is nothing left to say

I stare at my colored pencils bundled in a cup with their
sharpened colorful tips pointed in the air and it looks like
even they're giving praise to God

I accidentally left my gel ink pen in the pocket of my pants
it went through the washing machine and dryer and it
still wrote perfectly
now that's loyalty

BIOMIMETICS
Studying animals has inspired some inventions
behaving like animals has caused much suffering

Keep abusing alcohol and drugs
and you'll sleep next to strangers either in jail, rehab, or
the graveyard

If I manage to get at least one of my poems into your
house, then a proliferation begins.....
like bed bugs

Try to say loyal love 10 times in a row as fast as you can good, now try to show some

⁂

God let my resentments Melt Away like crayons left on a heated vent

⁂

The sound of grapes being crushed can instill fear into the hearts of some people

Before you play the race card just remember, cards should be shuffled

Before you formed an opinion about me I had already formed a fact about you

I heard that schools no longer teach kids to write in cursive but how will they learn about all the twists and turns that are coming their way

When you're in the vicinity of a poet your actions are being pondered

~※~

I know nothing about Xanax but I'm learning about Psalms 94:19

~※~

They drag the Dead Poet from his house leaving a trail of ink behind

Yes, I've got bullet wounds but you don't know about the bullets I've dodged

⁓※⁓

I've had my car stolen I've had my bicycle stolen but some have had their innocence taken away, so let me not complain

⁓※⁓

Oh don't get me wrong superheroes are cool but what if you need someone to save you from yourself

We're All Creatures of habit and if you have an addictive personality on top of that I'll pray for you

---

Because of Hope you can still crack a smile under trial although in a Mona Lisa Style

---

The irony is if you have an enlarged heart you are in danger but if you have a big heart you'll be blessed

Before the thief made it home with his stolen goods, a court in heaven had already convened

The flickrd ashes from a cigarette make the ants think it's Pompeii all over again

They say genius is relative to insanity, yes, great minds break alike

As a baby I would suck my thumb while pulling on people's ear lobes
now I tug on people's ears in a different way

Trying to make someone stay is exasperating, like killing two stones with one bird

Riding a bicycle as a child I learned about equilibrium
now as an adult I must a team that same balance

Even in traffic a Christ-like mentality is needed

The Eraser doesn't always completely remove with the pencil wrote, and a bad memory lingers

---

You think sulfuric acid is corrosive, look what resentment did to his internal organs

Love is.....chocolate, wine, orchids strawberries, puppies, violins

Pornography is..... maggots, cigarette butts broken glass, rat poison, nicotine, burnt bacon

If you had a broken heart then you should know how not to break another's heart

Never Enough salsa for the chips Never Enough cops for
the crime

⁂

If you still my identity you have to accept everything that
comes along with me

⁂

PARADISAIC VISIONS
the bicycles in Paradise will be lighter faster, stronger,
more comfortable,
and free

I know it's just cotton, but a brand new t-shirt makes me
feel like the son of Jor-el

A tiny bug flew into my eye,
a temporary discomfort for me, but a
new world for that insect

That old love letter of yours that you poured your heart
into is sitting on top of someone's desk being admired or
laughed at by people

PARADISAIC VISIONS

A child curiously stares at a rusty padlock as his father explains to him why I locks were needed in the old world

No,
that habit wasn't an addiction
but still a ferocious beast it was

The sound of a heartbreak is not
audible to human ears

Energy drinks are okay but holy spirit doesn't cause you to crash and contains no sugar

Energy drinks are okay but holy spirit doesn't cause you to crash and contains no sugar

If you abruptly stop reading my poetry expect severe withdrawal

It's no coincidence that words rhyme with other words thank you Lord

I should have stretched before I started this exercise in
futility

The weight bar in the gym holds heavy amounts of weight
every day but it never breaks
and there's nothing left to say

When my ink pens die I put them in a
Nike shoe box
a decent burial

Addictions need to be broken into fragments, not in halves, because two halves can easily be reassembled

PARADISAIC VISIONS-
that place that used to be a hospice is now a garden of lilacs we're a young lady goes to receive
poetic inspiration

False cliches fade away truthful
cliches are old and gray

Trying to legislate hate is like giving a candy apple to a
man whose toothless

My friend Vaughn bought me my first poem book
and now even he can't stop the verbal eruption

As I lay in bed
I vaguely can hear my ink pens discussing me

Continuing to shop with a shopping cart that has a bad wheel
this too is perseverance

He wears a crown embedded with eyeballs
because it's a royal pain being paranoid all the time

NEW NINEVEH-
If you had an orbital view of the earth you would see fire reaching out from some places. These areas are known as Detroit Chicago and District of Columbia. Cities where victims and villains are vice versa. And there are sections in the Middle East that give off radiant glows like the childhood game "lite brite"

They love to play God
but they don't want to imitate his love mercy and
forgiveness

And it turns out that even that sinister prong head Menace
was no match for an army of gentle suds and a cascade of
warm water

Even little children are wearing masks, there's a poem in
there somewhere but I just can't articulate it

BROOM SERVICE-

Years ago I observed and older coworker sweeping the floor like a meticulous scientist. I don't think a speck of dust escape the broom of this graceful bald-headed ballerina. This has become the cornerstone of my work ethic

I have received gifts and praises simply by offering people a glass of water
water is heavier than it looks

A lyricist meets the perfect dJ and beautiful music is made and so it is when a girl meets the man of her dreams

He said "don't worry about it, I've got bigger fish to fry"
but I didn't know he had to cook a Whale shark in a
greaseless skillet

"Well hello there my old friend"
said the voice of relapse

Wearing these masks make some people look suspicious,
but when they remove their masks and they still look
suspicious
be cautious

And there comes a time when a poet must look into his book and take his own advice

When a parasite works its way into the shell of a clam, the clam repeatedly produces a fluid to cover the irritant until a precious pearl is formed
when a poet is irritated by something his pen produces a fluid until a pearl of wisdom is formed

Reveal the light to them gradually, for fear they'll evaporate

If controlling your temper was an Olympic event, would you win gold, silver, bronze, or no medal at all

⁓※⁓

I wanted to get an expensive pair of basketball shoes that had a floral imprint on them, but I wondered what would people say, then I reminded myself that God created flowers and I put them on layaway

⁓※⁓

The projects in my head are far from being dilapidated

My Mom noticed all my books of poetry that I had in my
bedroom and she said
"I didn't know you had all of that inside your mind"
and at that very moment the tip of a giant Iceberg crashed
through my bedroom wall

BAPTISM DATES
A visible immersion solidifying and invisible conversion

I'm a legend in my own mind
and that's the safest place for me to be a legend

The Red Sun of Krypton subdues the powers of its people but when certain earthlings known as firefighters see a red Sun
their powers and abilities become super

The deepness of his meekness will make and atheist begin to reconsider

I told the lady bus driver what my real name was but she continues to call me Justice
should I remind her again, or just let it ride

Little do they know
about my ace in the Hole

FUHGETTABOUTIT-
I want pray to God in Italian, I said I was sorry for all
the wrong I've done, and he answered me back in Italian
and said
"f u h g g e t t a b o u t i t"

Or maybe the morning dew is the tears of angels who see
the violence in the city every night

The most comfortable blanket is knowing that you are loved

He cut so many corners I'm surprised he's still a (round)

Those who have sensitive hearts can sense everything

The good news is I have photographic memory the bad news is I have photographic memory

---

I left my book of poems open on purpose because I knew that you would look through it
and now I got you

When your tears start to smell like beer be in fear

I seen a racist person buying flowers for his wife you see he has love but he's just selective about who he shows it to

---

Lord protect me from the virus, not the submicroscopic ones but the ones with legs

---

Peter Parker was bitten by a spider and gained spider like abilities. I guess you must have been bitten by a weasel

THE SILENT ERROR

She consistently gives me the silent treatment so that's when I turned into Charlie Chaplin on her, and now here we are two silent figures moving around each other awkwardly

The face on the state of Montana is looking directly at the State of California being both mesmerized and surprised by its activities

CLEVERNESS

When traditional thoughts get escorted out of a Convention of unconventional thoughts

I don't know if he was blessed with
rhythm, but even Moses snapped

Being talked about is a part of life, being maliciously
gossiped about is a part of strife

Love and Kindness
guess which one is Batman and which one is Robin

My mind is so deep if you whisper your here and Echo

If someone tells you that you could be the poster child for Prozac, that's not a job offer

The reason I'm a vegan I don't believe in beefin

Not everybody owns a pet but everybody has a pet peeve

Sometimes it feels like there's bed bugs crawling on me even though they're not
psychological warfare is what these bugs are using

72 degrees would be the perfect outdoor temperature, not too hot not too cold, moderate and pleasant, and may it be that way with my temper

That statement you made is just like the last pair of underwear that I wore in "1994" .....
full of holes

<hr>

"I sit back and observe the whole scenery then nonchalantly tell you what it mean to me" -RAKIM

<hr>

Once God has liberated you from an addiction, only then will you party Like It's "1999"

I think I have pencil-phrenia,
voices come out of my head and exit through the lead

I cheer for the Denver Broncos, but I'm well-read like a
Chiefs fan

---

13 people killed in a Bomb Blast
25 people killed in mall shooting
4 people shot and killed at a nightclub
9 people killed in school shooting
50 people killed at a concert

The Flies stare in amazement at the way people are dropping

⁂

Somebody asked me "do you got a light dude" and I responded "yeah" but it'll blind you

⁂

He always likes to show his possessions. He's an apostrophe

The air that is forced out of my poetry book when I close it, could put out a California forest fire

---

You remind me of that movie with Denzel Washington and Julia Roberts
because you got more mouth than a pelican and you're never brief

---

Whenever I open up you'll fall into a sinkhole

You have a better chance of entering Fort Knox than you do Sam's Club if you're not a member

———※———

This world we live in is very cold make sure you dress in layers

———※———

Alienation,
No, not a race of
extraterrestrials but a condition you caused yourself for being overly righteous

I've never been married before
I have not had this privilege, but when I do receive this blessing, it's going to take God and two of his angels to pull me away from her

I heard someone say" I hate cilantro" and I thought to myself "what evil could this beautiful green herb have done to this individual"

Yellow and black
the colors of a mysteriously happy person

You should join the X-Men
because you have The Uncanny ability of keeping a
straight face while you lie to people

What's worse than the blind leading the blind? one know
it all leading another know it all

A Dazzle of zebras makes a prejudiced person worried

STATISTICS
They say that you are more likely to be murdered by someone of your own race or
by someone that you know
the bi-racial loner is envied

A Barber Shop can be a fertile breeding ground for some frivolous talk
but I am forced to listen to it because there is a man standing behind me with a razor to my throat

Only God can unite all races he solved the Rubik's cube
on his first try

Endurance
The only true form of insurance

That breeze you create when you walked by another
person is a strong indicator yes, your tail will tell the tale

In the near future God will have every nationality of mankind doing the Electric Slide

The Bible says you should love your enemy, but every time I wear a pair of Nike shoes with Adidas clothing I feel........
conflicted

Just because your past is checkered you can still go on to play chess

My favorite R&B group is a band called "Mint Condition"
but never may that describe the condition of my Bible

Even Muhammad Ali lost a couple of fights

Regarding your faith, even a sliver of soap can be a giver
of Hope

The beautiful voice of a black songstress
can make a racist persons tattoos begin to melt

I have a superhero complex, am I talkin about my
personality, or an actual building where us Heroes go
to write

After you are done reading this poem, turn around, I'm standing right behind the Moon

Some people are so fishy they flake with a fork

I try to keep my head up like I'm at an air show.

"And there's nothing left to say."

Printed in the United States
by Baker & Taylor Publisher Services